# MAKING YOUR
# M.A.R.K.

By Caleb Wesco

Erica Basora

Copyright © 2025 by Caleb Wesco, Erica Basora

All rights reserved. No part of this publication may be reproduced, distributed, or transmitted in any form or by any means, including photocopying, recording, or other electronic or mechanical methods, without the prior written permission of the publisher, except in the case of brief quotations embodied in critical reviews and specific other noncommercial uses permitted by copyright law.

For permissions, inquiries, speaking engagements, discounts for bulk orders, and schools or associations, contact:

lgmexp.com or email lgmexpbooks@gmail.com

Printed in the United States of America.

# CONTENTS

DEDICATION ................................................................. 5

ACKNOWLEDGMENTS .................................................. 6

INTRODUCTION: YOU ARE HERE ................................... 7

CHAPTER 1: EMBRACE THE UPS AND DOWNS ............... 10

    YOU'RE VALUABLE—THAT'S WHY IT FEELS SO HARD ........................ 11
    YOU'VE STILL GOT WORK TO DO .................................................... 11
    PEACE ISN'T THE ABSENCE OF PIECES ............................................. 12
    LET'S MAKE IT REAL – ASK YOURSELF ............................................. 13

CHAPTER 2: MOTIVATION — THE FIRE THAT STARTS THE JOURNEY .. 15

    WRITE THIS DOWN: M.A.R.K. ........................................................ 15
    THE TRUTH ABOUT MOTIVATION ................................................... 16
    PUT THE MAN TOGETHER .............................................................. 17
    YOU ARE THE KEY .......................................................................... 18
    DON'T WAIT FOR PERFECT ............................................................. 19
    MOTIVATION IS A MIRROR ............................................................. 19
    REFLECT & RESPOND ..................................................................... 20
    ACTION STEP: MAKE THE VOW ...................................................... 20

CHAPTER 3: ACTION — THE CURE FOR A.T.N.A. ............ 22

    ACTION IS A BEAUTIFUL THING ...................................................... 22
    ANALYSIS PARALYSIS ..................................................................... 23
    THE PSYCHOLOGICAL PANDEMIC ................................................... 24
    I REFUSE TO BE A.T.N.A. ................................................................ 25
    I REFUSE TO BECOME AN A.T.N.A. (POEM) .................................... 26
    GIVE YOURSELF CREDIT ................................................................. 27
    REFLECT & RESPOND ..................................................................... 27
    ACTION STEP: MAKE THE VOW ...................................................... 28

**CHAPTER 4 – RESILIENCE: YOU SURVIVED 100% OF YOUR WORST DAYS.29**
- YOU'VE ALREADY PROVEN YOU'RE STRONG ................................................. 30
- YOUR SECRET WEAPON ................................................................................. 31
- THE STRENGTH BEHIND THE STRUGGLE ....................................................... 31
- WHEN YOU FEEL LIKE QUITTING... ................................................................ 32
- THE RESILIENT SPIRIT .................................................................................... 33
- REFLECT & RESPOND ..................................................................................... 34
- ACTION STEP: MAKE THE VOW ..................................................................... 34

**CHAPTER 5: KNOWLEDGE — TURNING POTENTIAL INTO POWER ...... 35**
- POTENTIAL IS NOT POWER ........................................................................... 36
- YOU CAN'T JUST KNOW IT—YOU'VE GOT TO BE IT ..................................... 36
- THERE'S MORE FOR YOU .............................................................................. 37
- C.A.N.T. — CUT ALL NEGATIVE THINKING .................................................... 38
- F.A.I.T.H. — FEAR AIN'T IN THIS HOUSE ...................................................... 39
- REFLECT & RESPOND .................................................................................... 39
- ACTION STEP: MAKE THE VOW ..................................................................... 39

**CHAPTER 6: MAKE THE VOW, MAKE YOUR MARK ............................... 41**
- YOU'RE NOT WHO YOU WERE ...................................................................... 42
- THIS VOW IS YOUR TURNING POINT ............................................................ 42
- FINAL WORD OF ENCOURAGEMENT ............................................................ 43
- MAKE THE VOW ............................................................................................. 44
- YOUR MARK STARTS NOW ............................................................................ 44

**WHAT'S NEXT: LIVE IT OUT, WALK IT OUT ............................................. 46**
- THIS BOOK WAS A LAUNCHPAD .................................................................... 46
- WALK IN THE M.A.R.K. DAILY ........................................................................ 47
- FROM VOW TO LIFESTYLE ............................................................................. 48
- YOUR NEXT STEP IS THE MOST IMPORTANT ONE ....................................... 48
- YOUR FINAL REFLECTION .............................................................................. 49
- MAY THIS BE YOUR REALITY ......................................................................... 50
- BOOK CALEB WESCO TO SPEAK .................................................................... 50

**ABOUT THE AUTHOR ................................................................................. 52**

# Dedication

This book is dedicated to the 2020–2021 version of me—the one who almost gave up.

The me who lost his job got struck by life (literally—there was a car accident) and questioned everything... even the dream.

But even in that darkness, a light broke through.

It came in the form of a powerful reminder from my friend, Kathleen Stallard, who said:

**"Walk through what others are scared of to show them they can be brave too."**

So this is for that version of me—

The one who kept showing up.

The one who didn't quit.

The one who dared to dream again.

I see you. I thank you. I honour you.

Because of you, I'm here—

A speaker. An author. A purpose-driven force.

And to anyone reading this: you can put your name here too.

This is your permission slip. Your reminder.

You're not just here to survive.

You're here to make your M.A.R.K.

# Acknowledgments

To every soul who's ever wondered, *"Am I enough?"*—this one's for you.

Thank you to the friends, family, mentors, and fellow travellers who stood beside me when I couldn't stand alone.

Your belief gave me fuel.

Your prayers gave me power.

Your presence gave me peace.

Special thanks to every student, every audience member, and every reader who's ever shared a moment, a story, or a hug.

**You're the reason I keep showing up.**

Let's Get Motivated.

# Introduction: You Are Here

There will be moments in life when you feel like a nobody—
Or times when no one stops to remind you that you *are* somebody.

So before we go any further, let me be the one to say it loud and clear:

**You are somebody. And you matter.**

You matter because you've made it to a place I call *Here*.

*Here*, it might mean you're figuring out your next move.

It might mean you're standing on the edge of a breakthrough… or in the middle of a breakdown.

Maybe you're thriving—or perhaps you're barely surviving.

Whatever *Here* looks like for you, one thing's for sure:

**You're still standing. And that counts.**

Take a second.

Breathe in deep.

Now give yourself a pat on the back—because you've survived **100%** of your hardest days.

That's not luck.

That's **strength.**

That's **the purpose** of knocking on your door, asking:

"Are you ready to answer?"

Now listen—I know you want to live a *great* life.

But here's the truth:

**Being great is not the same as living with purpose.**

A purpose-driven life?

That's a life where you show up and **make your M.A.R.K.**

This book? It's not for people who love the sound of big dreams but never move their feet.

It's not for the folks suffering from **A.T.N.A.—All Talk, No Action.**

This is for the **doers.**

The **hungry ones.**

The **misfits** who know deep down they're built for *more.*

The ones who feel that tug in their chest that says:

"There's more in me—I just need the path to pull it out."

If that's you, let me ask:

Are you ready to move from great... to *purpose*?

Are you prepared to turn the page on your past and plant a flag in your future?

If you're nodding...

If something in you is stirring...

If your heart just whispered, "Let's go" —

**Then welcome.**

This journey is yours.

This book is your invitation.

Let's make your **M.A.R.K.**

# Chapter 1: Embrace the Ups and Downs

Hey—you.
Yeah, *you*'re reading this.
Let me tell you something up front:

If you're going through something right now…

That doesn't mean you're losing.

It means you're *alive*.

Ever seen a heart monitor?

That line going up and down? That's what life looks like.

The moment it goes flat?

That's not peace—that's a *problem*.

So don't curse the chaos.

Don't run from the lows.

Don't panic under pressure.

The ups and downs do you feel?

They're not signs of failure.

They're signs of **life.**

## You're Valuable—That's Why It Feels So Hard

Let me break it down:

Negativity only gets to you because there's something **valuable** inside you.

Think about it—

**Thieves don't break into empty houses.**

If life has been pressing you, testing you, piling on the pressure—

It's only because there's **treasure** within you.

Because pressure always surrounds **purpose.**


## You've Still Got Work to Do

If you woke up this morning, hear me clearly—

You've still got a mission.

God didn't put breath in your lungs today so you could drift through it.

There's a reason you're still here.

There's an assignment in your heartbeat.

You might not see the whole map yet, but trust this:

You are *not* an accident.

I don't care how messy your season looks.

I don't care how many setbacks you've had.

You're still **marked.**

You're still **chosen.**

You're still **needed.**


**Peace Isn't the Absence of Pieces**

You don't need a perfect life to walk in purpose.

Some of you are stuck because you're waiting to feel "ready."

You're saying, "I'll move forward once things calm down."

**Nah.**

"Peace is not the absence of hardship, hard work, or trouble.

Real peace is to be amid all these things and keep calm in your heart."

—Marcus Aurelius

Peace isn't about having it all together.

It's the decision to move forward *anyway.*

Your life might feel scattered.

But let me tell you something—

**God can do more with your *yes* than you could ever do with your perfection.**

Stop seeing yourself as broken glass.

Start seeing yourself as stained glass—

Still together.

Still powerful.

Still reflecting the light.

**Let's Make It Real – Ask Yourself:**

- What's the toughest thing I've faced lately—and what did it teach me?
- Am I letting challenging moments disqualify me from my purpose?
- What if even my *worst* day is still part of God's bigger plan?
- What's one piece of my life I'm ready to pick up today?

**Action Step: Make the Vow**

Write this down. Say it out loud if you have to:

"I'm not quitting because it's hard.

I'm growing because I'm still here.

I may be in pieces, but I still have peace.

I may be in a valley, but I am still marked for greatness.

I won't wait for perfect.

I will show up in purpose—flaws and all."

Now take a pen.

**Sign your name.**

**Write today's date.**

That moment right there?

That's the beginning of your **mark.**

# Chapter 2: Motivation – the Fire That Starts the Journey

Let's talk about something fundamental: **Motivation.**
That fire that gets you up in the morning.

The thing that pushes you when life tries to pull you down.

That's *why* behind your *what*.

Now let me say this upfront—

You're allowed to have bad days. Everybody has them.

But here's the key:

**Don't let your bad days have *you*.**

**Write This Down: M.A.R.K.**

If you've got a pen, write this down. This is the framework that'll take you from where you are to where you *want* to be:

- M – Motivation
- A – Action
- R – Resilience
- K – Knowledge

This is your blueprint. And it starts with the **M**...

So, let's dig into **motivation.**

**The Truth about Motivation**

Now, I'm not gonna lie to you. (Yeah, I said *gonna*.)

Some days, motivation comes easy.

You wake up feeling good. The sun's out. Bills are paid. Doors are opening.

But other days?

Motivation goes missing.

You've got to go looking for it.

Digging.

Clawing.

**Reminding yourself why you started.**

If you're having one of *those* days right now, hear me loud:

**You don't need to feel motivated to stay committed.**

You need to *choose* to keep showing up.

"Commitment is staying true to what you said you would do long after the mood you said it in has left."

—Inky Johnson

**Put the Man Together**

Let me tell you a story.

One Saturday morning, a little boy ran downstairs, full of energy.

He was ready to play, laugh, and spend time with his dad.

His dad?

Sitting at the table, sipping coffee and reading a *National Geographic* magazine.

"Dad! Can we play a game?" the boy asked.

Without looking up, the dad said, "No. I'm reading."

Again: "Dad, come on!"

Still, "No."

Once more.

Still—"No, son. This is *my* time."

But if you know kids, they don't give up that easily.

Finally, the dad had an idea. He tore out a page from the magazine—a picture of the Earth.

He ripped it into pieces and handed it to his son.

"Fine. Do you want a game? Put this back together."

The dad smirked, expecting 30 minutes of peace.

But within *30 seconds*, the boy shouted, "Done!"

The dad looked over—*shocked*.

Every continent is in place. The Earth? Perfectly assembled.

"How'd you finish so fast?" he asked.

The boy smiled and pointed to the glass table.

"Dad, on the back of the Earth picture... was a picture of a man.

So I figured... if I put the *man* together, I could put the *world* together."

That's motivation.

That's perspective.

That's **true.**

**You Are the Key**

Let me ask you something bold:

**What if *you* are the answer you've been waiting for?**

Not a new job.

Not a new relationship.

It's not some random stroke of luck.

**YOU.**

Many people are waiting for someone else to come and save them.

But what if the *rescue*... is already looking back at you in the mirror?

> "S_ccess can't be spelled without 'U.'"
>
> —Lurena Cobb

You're not a background character in someone else's story.

You're the **main event** on your own.

You have the power to shift legacies.

But it starts with **motivation.**

Not just a spark—but a decision.

### Don't Wait for Perfect

If you're waiting for everything to be perfect, you'll be waiting *forever.*

Some of you are stuck in the "when I..." loop:

"When I get more money..."

"When I feel more confident..."

"When I have more time..."

Let me give it to you straight:

**Motivation doesn't always show up first.**

Sometimes, it shows up *after* you move.

You take one step—and suddenly, the energy comes.

You say "yes,"—and your spirit catches fire.

You show up scared—but consistent—and things start to shift.

### Motivation Is a Mirror

Motivation isn't about hype. It's not about applause.

**Validation is only suitable for parking.**

True motivation? It's internal. It's *vision-driven*.

So ask yourself:

- What's pushing me?
- What's pulling me?
- What am I willing to let go of... to become who I was born to be?

"Life is like a mirror—it will only reflect what you put in front of it."

—Unknown

Motivation isn't about what you *achieve*.

It's about who you *become*.

### ⌂ Reflect & Respond

- What's driving me right now—and is it strong enough to last when it gets hard?
- Am I waiting to *feel* motivated... instead of *choosing* to be?
- Who am I doing this for—and is that reason strong enough to wake me up every morning?

### ✓ Action Step: Make the Vow

Let's read these affirmations together:

"I will stop waiting to feel ready.

I will move even if I feel unsure.

I don't need a perfect plan—I need to start.

I will stay motivated not by the noise around me,

but by the purpose inside me."

Now sign it. Date it.

Then walk over to the mirror, look yourself in the eyes, and say: **"Let's Get Motivated."**

# Chapter 3: Action – the Cure for A.T.N.A.

Now that you've found your fire, it's time to **move**. Because motivation without action, that's like a car with no gas.

It looks good… but it's going nowhere.

You can be inspired all day long,

But until you act, **nothing changes.**

This is the "A" in **M.A.R.K.**

**A is for Action.**

This is the moment when your *inspiration becomes impact.*

Because you can dream it, believe it, even pray over it…

But you're still stuck in the same place if you don't do something.

**Action Is a Beautiful Thing**

**Action** is a verb.

It means movement.

It means progress.

It means going from where you *are*... to where you *want* to be.

Most of us don't struggle with dreaming big—

We struggle with **starting small.**

We get stuck.

Overthinking.

Overplanning.

Overanalyzing.

We say "one day"...

And "one day" becomes **no day.**

**Analysis Paralysis**

There's a name for that freeze. It's called **analysis paralysis.**

You know the feeling—your brain is full of ideas, dreams, and visions...

But your feet won't move.

Why?

Because somewhere deep down, a voice is whispering:

- "You're not ready."
- "What if you fail?"
- "Who do you think you are?"

And sometimes it's not just the inner voice...

It's the **outside noise**, too.

People saying:

- "The wall's too high."
- "The gap's too wide."
- "The climb's too steep."

But let me tell you something:

**One immediate action means more than a thousand good intentions.**

You don't need 1,000 plans.

You need **one decision.**

You don't need a complete strategy.

You need **one step.**

The bridge from where you are to where you're going?

It's **made of movement.**


**The Psychological Pandemic**

There's a pandemic out there—and I'm not discussing COVID.

I'm talking about a *psychological* pandemic.

It's silent.

It's sneaky.

It's **deadly to your purpose.**

It's called **A.T.N.A.**

**All. Talk. No. Action.**

Do you know what that looks like?

- Big dreams... but bigger distractions.
- Powerful thoughts... but no follow-through.
- Constant complaining... but no change.
- Getting hyped... and doing nothing.

**That's A.T.N.A.**

And the truth is—we've *all* caught it at some point.

But **today?**

We break the cycle.

**I Refuse to Be A.T.N.A.**

Say this with me:

**I refuse to be All Talk, No Action.**

I refuse to sit on the sidelines of my own life.

I refuse to clap for everybody else while my purpose collects dust.

I refuse to suffer from the potential that never turns into power.

Because I'm climbing the mountain.

And here's what that looks like:

**I Refuse to Become an A.T.N.A. (Poem)**

I refuse to become an A.T.N.A.

What's that? All talk and no action.

Big dreams... but bigger distractions.

Always crying over what didn't happen?

Inspired thoughts—but no reaction?

Nah.

I'm shaking myself from standing still.

I'm chasing purpose, even if it's uphill.

This mountain of success—I choose to climb.

Following the beat of ambition in my heart, soul, and mind.

"Impossible" won't be my excuse or delay.

I'm on track. I'm locked in. I'm here to stay.

Because I refuse to be A.T.N.A.

That's All Talk. No Action. No way.

From now on, I'll eliminate distractions.

Put power behind my passions.

Inspired thoughts followed by bold decisions.

I raised my hands on "Goal Hill" with a vision.

And when I look back on the mountain of success,

I'll say, "You did it."

But this is only the *first* win—so stick with it.

I'm **motivated**, **dedicated**, down-right activated...

Because I *refuse* to become an A.T.N.A. again.

**Give Yourself Credit**

You may not be where you want to be...

But listen—you're *miles* ahead of the person still sitting on the couch.

You're taking steps.

You're choosing movement.

It's not all at once.

It's **one step at a time.**

So, give yourself some credit.

And then?

**Keep moving forward.**

**✑Reflect & Respond**

- Where in my life have I been "All Talk, No Action"?
- What's one simple step I can take *today* toward my goal?
- What excuses do I need to shut down so I can finally rise?

### ✓ Action Step: Make the Vow

Write this down. Say it if you need to.

"I will no longer be All Talk, No Action.

I will not overthink myself into stillness.

I will move, even when I'm unsure.

One step is better than no step.

I am not stuck.

I'm just getting started."

Now sign it. Date it.

Then, do *one small thing* that moves you forward **today**.

Send the email.

Make the call.

Draft the plan.

**Start.**

# Chapter 4 – Resilience: You Survived 100% of Your Worst Days

We've lit the fire.

We've started to move.

Now it's time to talk about what *keeps you going*—especially when life gets heavy.

Let's talk about what separates the people who **quit**...

from the people who **conquer.**

It's not talent.

It's not connections.

It's not luck.

It's **resilience.**

The power to keep going—even when everything in you says stop.

The decision to stay in the game—even when the scoreboard looks bad.

The strength to say, "I might bend, but I won't break."

This is the "R" in your **M.A.R.K.** framework.

Because when motivation fades...

When action feels heavy...

**Resilience** steps in and says:

"We're not finished yet."

And before we go any further, let me drop this truth:

**"Life doesn't happen *to* you—**

**It happens *to* you...**

**To bring the best out of you."**

**You've Already Proven You're Strong**

If I could sit down with you right now and hear your story...

You could tell me some stuff.

You've been through dark days.

You've fought silent battles.

You've survived storms that would've taken someone else out.

And guess what?

**You made it here.**

I don't know what *there* looked like for you...

But I know this:

You **survived** there.

And now you're *here*.

You've survived **100%** of your worst days.

You may not feel like a superhero...

But that's precisely what you are.

That's resilience.

**Your Secret Weapon**

Do you want to know your cheat code?

Your unfair advantage?

It's not that you never fall.

It's that you **keep getting back up.**

Because when other people stop at *hard,*

You say, "**Watch me.**"

When others quit in the dark,

**You shine brighter.**

Your ability to keep showing up—when everything tells you not to?

That's not just survival.

That's **a superpower.**

That's the kind of resilience that turns pressure into purpose…

And pain into power.

**The Strength Behind the Struggle**

Sometimes, the hard seasons don't come to destroy you.

Sometimes, they come to **reveal you.**

Maybe you weren't weak—

Maybe you were already strong...

And the storm just made you **prove it.**

The dark days didn't break you.

**They built you.**

"My dark days made me strong. Or maybe I already was strong, and they made me prove it."

—Emery Lord

Now you've got the *receipts.*

You've got the proof that making your M.A.R.K. isn't just something you say—

**It's something you live.**

**When You Feel Like Quitting...**

There will be days when you feel like quitting.

When it's all uphill.

When your smile feels fake.

When your strength feels spent.

But hear this:

"When things go wrong, as they sometimes will,

When the road you're trudging seems all uphill,

When the funds are low, and the debts are high,

And you want to smile, but you have to sigh,

When care is pressing you down a bit...

Rest, if you must, but **don't you quit.**"

—Edgar Guest

**Rest if you must...**

But don't you *dare* quit?

Don't quit on your goals.

Don't quit on your purpose.

Don't quit on *you*.

Resilience got you this far.

And resilience will take you **the rest of the way.**


**The Resilient Spirit**

Your bounce-back game?

**Unmatched.**

You've been knocked down—but never knocked out.

You've smiled through the pain.

You've cried through victory.

You've walked into rooms where you didn't feel ready—

but you *owned the space anyway.*

You are **living proof** that resilience is real.

So the next time life presses in, remember:

**You've been through worse. And you're still standing.**

### ✍Reflect & Respond

- What's something I made it through that I didn't think I would?
- When was the last time I wanted to quit—but didn't?
- How has resilience shaped who I am today?

### ✅ Action Step: Make the Vow

Say it out loud.

Write it down.

"I have survived 100% of my worst days.

I am not built to break.

I may feel pressure, but I will not fold.

I will rest when I need to—but I will never quit.

I am resilient. And I will keep going."

Sign it.

Date it.

That vow?

That's your **backbone** on the hard days.

# Chapter 5: Knowledge — Turning Potential into Power

We've reached the final piece of the **M.A.R.K.** framework. You've been motivated.

You've taken action.

You've walked through fire—and come out with resilience.

But this last piece?

This is the one that **multiplies** everything.

**K is for Knowledge.**

Not just what you read in books.

Not just facts and figures.

We're talking about *applied wisdom*.

**The truth that transforms.**

The kind of knowledge that turns *lessons into lifestyle*.

That takes what life *taught* you—and uses it to change the world.

**Potential Is Not Power**

Let's get something clear:

**Knowledge is not power.**

Knowledge is **potential** power.

It becomes *real* power only when it's:

- ✅ Organized into a plan
- ✅ Pointed toward a goal
- ✅ Fueled by action

So many people walk around knowing *exactly* what to do…

But never do it.

They're packed with potential—

But *nothing's happening.*

That's like owning a toolbox complete with powerful tools…

And never building a thing.

It's not enough to know what's possible.

You've got to *use* what you know

To build what you were *made* for.

**You Can't Just Know It—You've Got to Be It**

Let me say it straight:

**Don't settle for knowing you could be successful.**

Move into actually *being* successful.

Stop replaying lessons in your head—

And start activating them in your *life*.

Take what you've been through…

What you've learned…

What you've survived…

And let that be the **fuel** for what you do *next*.

**There's More For You**

If there's one thing I know for sure, it's this:

**There's more out there for you.**

More opportunity.

More growth.

More purpose.

Don't let where you've been limit where you can go.

Don't let what you've seen be the ceiling for what you can build.

You haven't seen your best yet.

You haven't learned your last lesson.

And you *definitely* haven't done your most excellent work.

There's more inside of you—

And now?

It's time to **activate it.**

## C.A.N.T. — Cut All Negative Thinking

Let's talk to that voice in your head.

The one that says:

"I can't do this."

"I'm not ready."

"It's too late."

Let's redefine "can't."

It doesn't mean *I cannot.*

It means: **Cut All Negative Thinking.**

Cut the doubt.

Cut the Fear.

Cut the excuses.

Cut the self-sabotage.

Because when you cut off negative thoughts:

Your **faith** rises

Your **clarity** sharpens

Your **action** becomes powerful

**That's how you win.**

## F.A.I.T.H. — Fear Ain't In This House

Now let me spell something out:

**F.A.I.T.H. = Fear Ain't In This House.**

You've come too far.

You've fought through too many nights.

You've carried too many lessons to let Fear live in you now.

You've got the knowledge.

Now, walk in the **faith** to apply it.

Don't just carry wisdom—**live** it.

Don't just collect insight—**use** it.

Don't just hold on to lessons—**let them lead you.**

### ✎ Reflect & Respond

- What knowledge from my life have I been sitting on instead of applying?
- What plan of action can I create from what I already know?
- What negative thoughts do I need to cut today?

### ✓ Action Step: Make the Vow

Write this down. Own it:

"I will not sit on potential—I will **activate** it.

I will turn what I know into how I grow.

I will cut all negative thinking.

I will live by faith.

I will organize my knowledge into action.

Because **Fear ain't in this house**—and **success is.**"

Now sign it.

Date it.

Speak it out loud if you need to.

**This is your shift.**

This is your *activation moment.*

# Chapter 6: Make the Vow, Make Your Mark

You've made it *here*.
And *here* isn't just a place on a page—

It's a place in your *spirit*.

It's a moment of *decision*.

You've seen the blueprint:

- **M** - You found your **motivation** and learned that the heartbeat of your purpose begins with *you*.

- **A** - You took **action** and broke free from being *All Talk, No Action*.

- **R** - You embraced **resilience** and remembered that you've survived *100%* of your worst days.

- **K** - You unlocked the power of **knowledge**, turning potential into plans and truth into transformation.

Now it's time.

It's time to stop waiting for the right moment.

It's time to stop waiting for *permission*.

Time to take everything you've learned—

And do the one thing that separates **dreamers** from **doers**:

**Make the vow.**

**You're Not Who You Were**

You started this journey looking for a spark.

Maybe you came in uncertain. Hesitant. Wounded.

But look at you *now*.

You've been **ignited.**

You've been **equipped.**

You've been **activated.**

So no—you're not who you were at the beginning of this book.

You're becoming who you were always *meant* to be.

**This Vow Is Your Turning Point**

A vow is more than a statement.

It's a **line in the sand.**

A **flag in the ground.**

A **covenant** between your present and your future.

It's you saying:

"I will not go back to who I was

before I knew what I'm capable of."

It's you saying:

"I will not sit on my potential—

I will release it."

It's you saying:

**"I will make my M.A.R.K."**

### Final Word of Encouragement

Before we make this official, let me leave you with something I said at the end of my talk:

**"May the best days of your past**

**be the worst days of your future."**

That means the goodness *ahead* of you

It is greater than anything *behind* you.

It means you're not done.

You're just getting started.

So what now?

You **take** the vow.

You **live** the vow.

You **become** the vow.

And then?

**You make your mark.**

**Make the Vow**

Right here. Right now. Say it. Write it. *Own* it.

"I vow to live on purpose.

I vow to stay motivated, take action, build resilience, and apply what I know.

I vow to stop shrinking, hiding, and hesitating.

I vow to speak up, show up, and rise.

I vow to stop waiting for the perfect moment—

And start making every moment count.

I vow to make my mark—

For myself, for my legacy, for my God."

**Signed:** _____

**Date:** _____

**Your Mark Starts Now**

You have what it takes.

You've *always* had it.

But now you've got the **vision**...

The **framework**...

The **fire.**

So make your mark:

In your **home.**

In your **business.**

In your **ministry.**

In your **generation.**

Because the world isn't waiting for another expert.

**It's waiting for *you*.**

The real you. The bold you. They called you.

**Let's go.**

# What's Next: Live It Out, Walk It Out

So now you've done the reading. You've made the vow.

You've felt the call, found the fire—and *faced yourself*.

So... what's next?

Now you **walk it out.**

Because fundamental transformation doesn't happen in the margins of a book.

It happens in the **everyday moments** of your life.

**This Book Was a Launchpad**

The **Make Your M.A.R.K.** framework was never meant to sit on your shelf.

This wasn't about hype.

This was about **preparation**.

You weren't just reading—

You were *arming yourself.*

You were *training* for the next level.

You were *building* your inner leader.

Now it's time to **live like it.**

You're no longer just hoping for your future—

You're *holding the tools to build it.*

So what's next?

- It's the bold conversation you've been avoiding.
- It's the application you were too afraid to submit.
- It's the book you were born to write.
- It's the vision you've prayed about but haven't moved on.

What's next is already inside you—

**Waiting to be awakened.**


## Walk in the M.A.R.K. Daily

Your journey didn't end when you closed the last chapter.

It **just started.**

Now you've got a framework for how to live:

- **M – Motivation**: Start each day with purpose.
- **A – Action**: Do something—big or small—that moves you forward.
- **R – Resilience**: Keep going, even when it gets tough.
- **K – Knowledge**: Don't just learn—*live what you know.*

Pray through it.

Speak it over yourself.

Use it like a compass.

Let it become how you move.

How you think?

How you live.

**From Vow to Lifestyle**

You didn't just make a vow for a moment.

You made a vow to **shift the rest of your life.**

So when life tries to make you forget who you are—

**Go back to that vow.**

Let it anchor you.

Let it revive you.

Because you were **built to make an impact.**

You were **designed for legacy.**

You were **called to shift atmospheres.**

**Your Next Step Is the Most Important One**

You don't need to figure out all the steps right now.

You need to take **one.**

Because your next level doesn't require perfect conditions—

It requires a **willing heart** and a **faithful step.**

Progress isn't about speed.

It's about **direction.**

So what's next?

You move.

You build.

You become.

You make your mark—

With your story.

With your life.

With your faith.

## ✍ Your Final Reflection

- What's the first step I can take *to* walk out my vow today?
- Where do I need to be bold in applying the **M.A.R.K.** framework?
- What does "making my mark" look like in *this* season of my life?

**May This Be Your Reality**

"May the best days of your past...

Be the worst days of your future."

That's not just a beautiful closing line.

It's a **prophetic declaration**.

Your future is full of **impact**.

Your best days haven't even happened yet.

Your legacy is only just beginning.

So from this moment forward...

Don't just *carry* this book—

**Become it.**

Now...

**Go make your mark.**


Congratulations! You've made it this far.

If you're reading this, chances are you have a story within you—a book waiting to be written, a message waiting to be shared. Don't let fear or uncertainty hold you back any longer.

I encourage you to take the next step and connect with my publishing partner, That's Love Publishing. They specialize in helping first-time authors like you bring their stories to life and will walk with you through every step of the publishing process.

You can reach out directly at erica@thatslovepublishing.com or visit www.thatslovepublishing.com to learn more.

Your story matters. It's time to make your MARK.

**Book Caleb Wesco to Speak**

Thank you for reading *Make Your M.A.R.K.*

We hope this message lit a fire in you to step boldly into your purpose.

Want **Caleb Wesco** to speak at your school, organization, church, or next event?

✉@ email: **lgmexpbooks@gmail.com**

📱 Scan this QR Code for the official Making Your M.A.R.K one sheet and private Facebook list!

Caleb brings energy, truth, and fundamental strategies for growth, purpose, and impact.

Whether it's a room full of students or seasoned professionals, his mission remains the same:

**To help every person make their mark.**

# About the Author

Caleb Wesco is a passionate motivational speaker, youth leader, and author known for his dynamic presence, authentic storytelling, and ability to move audiences from doubt to action. Through years of keynote speaking and coaching, Caleb has inspired thousands to rise above their limitations and step into purpose-driven living.

He is the author of the children's book *ABC's to success*, which introduces young readers to foundational success principles with heart and clarity. Whether leading workshops, mentoring future leaders, or speaking to rooms full of dreamers, Caleb's mission is clear: to help people of all ages make their mark on the world.

Follow Caleb's journey and connect at:

**Instagram:** @calebwesco
**Facebook:** @calebwesco
**Youtube:** @calebwesco
**Linkedin:** Caleb Wesco
**X:** @calebwesco

Made in the USA
Middletown, DE
18 February 2026

28629643R00031